SELF-REGU
CONTROLLING IMPULSES

CONTENT & ACTIVITIES
A BOOK FOR
PARENTS AND CHILDREN

SELF-REGULATION

Welcome to Book Self-Regulation: Controlling Impulses

Hey there, my young adventurer!
Today, we're going to learn about something super cool called "self-regulation." It's like having a special power to be the boss of our emotions and feelings, just like how we control a remote for our favorite TV show.

Imagine you're playing your favorite game, and suddenly, you lose a level. It's totally okay to feel upset, and that's where self-regulation comes to the rescue! Take a deep breath, count to three, and remind yourself that it's okay to feel disappointed, but you can try again and do even better next time.

Sometimes, when things don't go as planned, we might feel angry or frustrated. That's when self-regulation steps in like a wise friend. Instead of lashing out or yelling, take a moment to understand why you feel that way. Maybe talking to a grown-up or taking a little break can help you feel better.

Self-regulation is like a special toolkit we carry with us everywhere. When we feel worried or anxious, we can open our toolkit and find things that soothe us, like taking a walk outside, drawing, or playing with a favorite toy.

Remember, my little explorer, self-regulation is all about being kind to ourselves and others. It's okay to have big feelings, but knowing how to handle them helps us make good choices and stay calm, just like a brave captain steering a ship through stormy waters.

So, the next time you face a tricky situation or feel overwhelmed, remember you have the amazing power of self-regulation. Use it like a magical compass to guide you to a place of calmness and understanding. With self-regulation by your side, you'll be ready to conquer any adventure that comes your way!

Self-Regulation - The Superpower Within!

Once upon a time, in a land of big feelings and exciting adventures, there lived a group of young superheroes. Each one had a special power related to their emotions. Meet Ben, the Self-Regulation Superhero!

Self-regulation is like having your very own superpower, dear readers. It's all about being the boss of your feelings and making wise choices. Imagine you have a magic remote control for your emotions. With self-control, you can press pause or play when you feel angry, sad, or even overly excited.

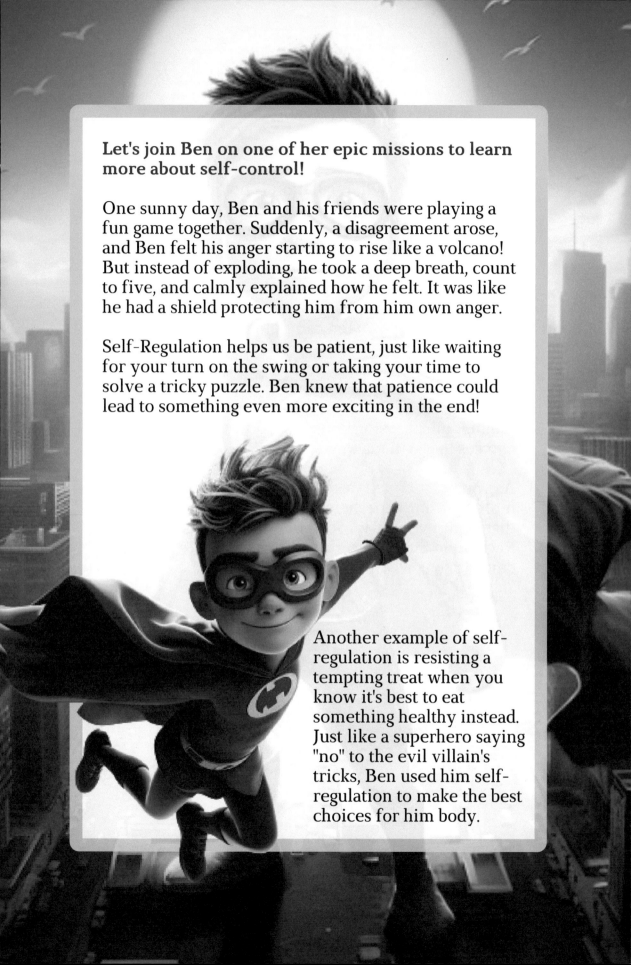

Let's join Ben on one of her epic missions to learn more about self-control!

One sunny day, Ben and his friends were playing a fun game together. Suddenly, a disagreement arose, and Ben felt his anger starting to rise like a volcano! But instead of exploding, he took a deep breath, count to five, and calmly explained how he felt. It was like he had a shield protecting him from him own anger.

Self-Regulation helps us be patient, just like waiting for your turn on the swing or taking your time to solve a tricky puzzle. Ben knew that patience could lead to something even more exciting in the end!

Another example of self-regulation is resisting a tempting treat when you know it's best to eat something healthy instead. Just like a superhero saying "no" to the evil villain's tricks, Ben used him self-regulation to make the best choices for him body.

Self-Regulation - The Superpower Within!

But guess what? Self-regulation is not just about saying "no." It's also about saying "yes" to the right things! When Ben needed to focus on him homework, he imagined he had laser-sharp eyes like a superhero. He ignored distractions and zoomed in on him tasks, completing them in record time!

Now, my young, you too can unlock the power of self-regulation! When you feel your emotions starting to bubble up, take a deep breath, count to three, and think about the best way to respond. Remember, it's okay to feel all kinds of emotions, but being the boss of your feelings means using your superpower to make choices that will make you proud!

As you practice self-regulation, you'll become an even more amazing superhero, able to face any challenge that comes your way. So, let your inner Self-Regulation Superhero shine bright, and let's save the day with our wise and thoughtful choices!

PARENTS, NOW IT'S UP TO YOU.

What can you do to teach children emotional education and self-regulation?

Check the list below to find out what you can do.

1. Help the child to calm down
Record this: the smaller the child, the more emotion he is. .
This is because the emotion comes from "the factory" - our basic emotions are born with us.
The emotions stayed with us because they helped us to survive in the evolutionary process. The emotions we feel inform us that something is happening in the environment and prepare our bodies for action.
So reinforcement: the smaller the child, the more emotion he is - his brain is not mature enough to understand more complex emotions.

2. Help the child to perceive and name his emotion
We help the child to perceive his or her emotional state and that of the other, in addition to naming the identified emotion.

3. Talk about that feeling
After the child is calm and has named his emotion, we talk about the emotion he is feeling.

4. Plan the actions
We lend our mature brain to help the child to think about the consequences.
Again: due to his cerebral immaturity, the child is unable to identify the consequences of his behaviors.
That's why we "borrow" our adult brain - we show the consequences of our actions and explain that our behavior affects others as well.

Self-regulation brings several benefits to different areas of life:

1)The child who learns from an early age to regulate his emotions develops a greater positive sense of himself, and this consequently develops in him a feeling of satisfaction and happiness,

2) She is more able to pay attention, focus and concentration are strengthened,

3) Has higher school performance,

4) Is more behaved, affectionate and confident,

5) Get along much better with other children and adults,

6) Has greater ability to resolve any conflict with friends with peace of mind,

7) Is less likely to act on impulse or anger,

8) Does not suffer from child stress and is not a victim of imaginary fears.

REGULATIONS

The marshmallow test

In 1972, Walter Mischel carried out the marshmallow experiment, in which he followed the children for a long time.

This experiment consisted of taking the child to a table with a marshmallow in front of him and explaining that he could eat that marshmallow or wait for the adult to return to eat it - that way, he would get a second marshmallow.

Mischel found that children who tolerated uncomfortable emotions and had the self-regulation to resist the marshmallow became more stable adults.

Still, it was found that these adults were healthier, with low involvement in crime, low obesity and good work and academic performance.

CHALLENGE

Challenge for parents and children.

- Let's put some marshmallows (if you think your child likes something else, you can use it) on a plate and leave it in front of your child for 20 minutes.

- You will ask him not to touch or eat.

- Try to watch his reaction without him noticing.

5 steps to manage your intense emotions

3 use words to say how you feel.

2 breathe deeply 3 times.

4 ask for help to solve the problem.

1 remember that it is wrong to hurt another.

5 count to 10 before any action.

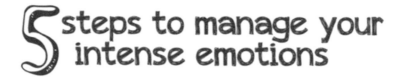

KeyWords
EDUCATION

WORD SEARCH

```
S E L F C O N T R O L F J U S Z C
Y C G R P G L R I P O M K U T S N
Z O N R A Y J G W Y X G R F O G T
Z O G K E F Y C F K O S W Q P H H
X F E Z M F D D K N H Y E A Z K C
E W T J Y W R X T R X X X K X K V
B R Y O N Z C Y U D M I F Q U A J
H T O D O G H V T L J D V R Q N M
Q T C Y V N O E E I K H L T J N Z
F H J T J I O M D E C I S I O N S
S I A E H Z S Z U L C C R G N V H
P N B U L M I L B K A H P O C Z O
X K G H P W N T C I U O P D O D G
W Z O G Q B G S M L T I U L L A V
W P O W E R E W K O I C R Y I T Z
F N D A K A F V X W O E I R O Q X
W I S E X D I T D K N S T K Z D R
```

choices	power	decisions
wise	stop	godly
choosing	selfcontrol	think
caution		

THE TRAFFIC LIGHT TECHNIQUE TO INCREASE CHILDREN'S SELF-REGULATION

TRAFFIC LIGHT OF EMOTIONS

Semaphore or traffic light is used to control the movement of cars on city streets.

What if we could also control our behavior?

Help painting the traffic light of the emotions below and observe the directions of each sign:

 Stop, think and breathe before you act

 Attention to emotions and thoughts

 Positive thinking to move on

Traffic Light of Emotions helps you to pay attention to the signals of the body and the environment! When something makes you angry, STOP and THINK before acting. So you can choose the best way to go!

DRAW A PICTURE OR TALK TO YOUR PARENTS ABOUT HOW YOU FEEL WHEN YOU GET VERY ANGRY AND FEEL LIKE YOU'RE LOSING CONTROL.

FIND 10 DIFFERENCES

LET'S PAINT, KIDS!

LET'S HELP OUR SUPERHEROE TO GET OUT OF THE MAZE.

Dear,

As we come to the end of this transformative journey through the pages of "Self-Regulation: Controlling Impulses," I want to express my heartfelt gratitude to each and every one of you.

To the young minds who eagerly soaked up the lessons and engaged with the activities, I commend your curiosity and enthusiasm. You've shown that learning about self-control can be an exciting adventure, and your dedication to the activities has undoubtedly planted the seeds for a future filled with self-awareness and emotional intelligence.

To the parents and caregivers who walked hand in hand with their children through this journey, your commitment to fostering a strong foundation of self-regulation is commendable. By participating in the activities and discussions, you've not only imparted valuable life skills but have also forged deeper connections with your children.

Remember that self-regulation is not a destination but an ongoing process. The tools and insights you've gained within these pages are meant to be lifelong companions. Embrace the journey ahead with open hearts and curious minds, for the path to self-mastery is one of continuous learning and growth.

Thank you for allowing me to be a part of your journey toward nurturing self-regulation. May your lives be filled with self-awareness, empathy, and the joy of embracing the full spectrum of human emotions while maintaining balance and control.

With gratitude and warm wishes,
Fabiano Rodrigues
KeyWords Education

Made in United States
Troutdale, OR
01/11/2025

27854765R00019